Lunar Jim
Bumper Fun!

BBC
CHILDREN'S BOOKS

BBC CHILDREN'S BOOKS
Published by the Penguin Group
Penguin Books Ltd, 80 Strand, London, WC2R 0RL, England
Penguin Group (USA) Inc., 375 Hudson Street, New York, New York 10014, USA
Penguin Group (Australia) Ltd, 250 Camberwell Road, Camberwell, Victoria 3124,
Australia (a division of Pearson Australia Group Pty Ltd)
Canada, India, New Zealand, South Africa
Published by BBC Children's Books, 2007
10 9 8 7 6 5 4 3 2 1

ISBN: 978-1-40590-292-2
Printed in China

Contents

Welcome to Moona Luna!

Colour in the Lunar gang!

Jim's true or false

Look at the picture of Jim and say whether these statements are true or false.

1. Jim has brown hair.
2. Jim's Lunar Scrambler is blue.
3. Rover is riding with Jim.
4. Jim is wearing his helmet.
5. Rover is wearing a helmet, too.

Answers: 1. False, Jim has yellow hair.
2. True, Jim's Lunar Scrambler is blue.
3. True, Rover is riding with Jim. 4.
True, Jim is wearing his helmet. 5.
False, Rover is not wearing a helmet.

Roving Rover

Rover is lost! Help him find his way through the maze and back to Jim.

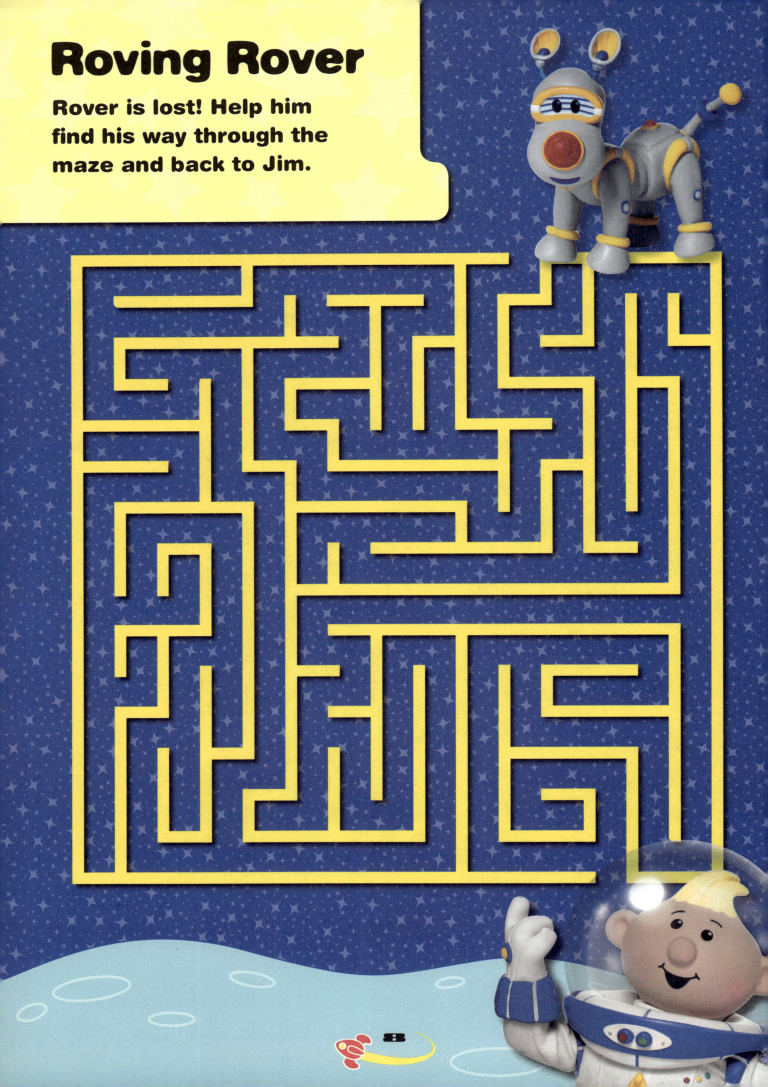

Cosmic colours: blue

There are many blue things to be found in Moona Luna. Look at these pictures and circle the ones that are blue.

How many blue things can you find in your house?

Answer: The following things are blue - Jim's Lunar Scrambler, the Lunar Fluffy, the Lunar plant and parts of Jim's space suit.

Who's hiding?

Can you tell who is hiding in the lunar landscape?

Answers: Jim is behind the moon mountains; T.E.D. is behind a stack of rocks by the cave; Ripple is in the cave; Rover is in a crater; Colby is behind a blue rock in front of the cave; Eco is at the front on the left-hand side.

Meet the gang

Colour these pictures of Jim and his friends.

Eco
Ripple

Space wordsearch

There are five space words hidden up and down and from side to side in this wordsearch.

Can you find them?

Moon

Star **Rocket** **Space** **Lunar**

R	R	X	T	S	P	A	C	E
O	C	L	K	F	P	O	I	J
C	D	A	L	U	N	A	R	M
K	S	M	S	I				
E	R	O	C	S				
T	E	O	G					
A	L	N	T					
S	T	A	R					
Y	W	F	K					

Memory game

Look carefully at all the things Colby has collected, then turn over the page and see if you can see what is missing.

What's missing?

Look at Colby's collection again. Can you tell what has gone?

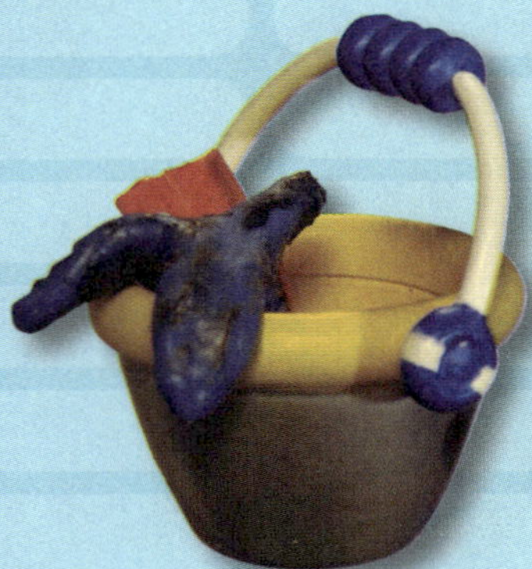

Answer: Ripple's Music Player and her Scanner, the Lunar Fluffy and the purple flower are missing.

Dot-to-dot

Join the dots to see what Jim uses to fly through space.

Hang on T.E.D.!

Colour in this picture of Jim, T.E.D. and Rover.

Lunar finger puppets

Create your own lunar adventures with these finger puppets of Jim and the gang.

You will need:
Round-ended scissors
Safe glue or sticky tape
Colouring pencils or crayons
A grown-up to help

1. Colour in the puppets of Jim and his friends.
2. Ask a grown-up to help you carefully cut them out along the dotted lines.
3. Bend the two sides of each puppet around and stick them together with safe glue or sticky tape. Do this for each puppet, then wait for the glue to dry.
4. Put the puppets on your fingers and get lunar!

glue

glue

glue

glue

glue

String trail

Jim has found a piece of string. Help him follow the trail and see who it leads to.

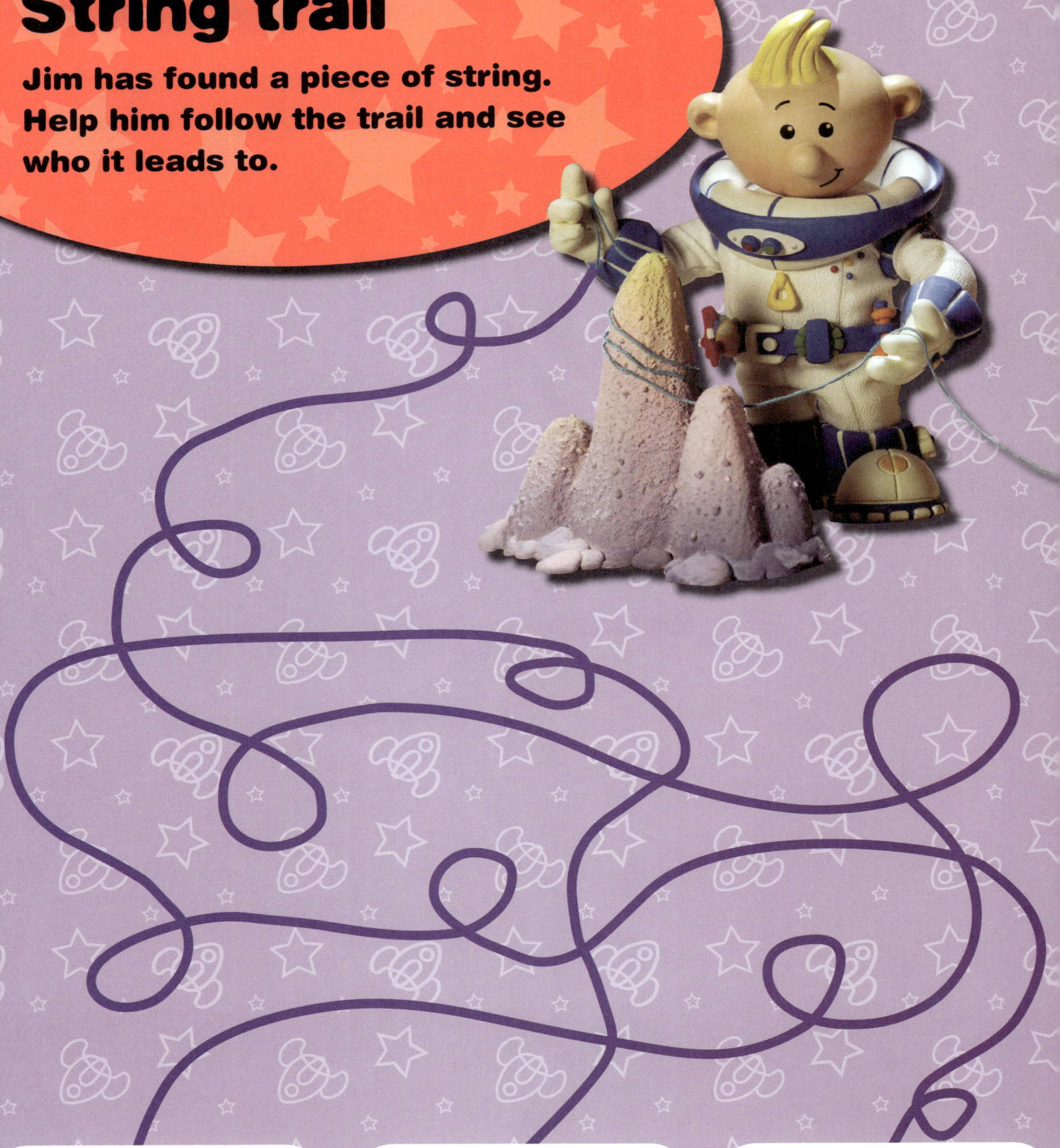

Answer: Ripple

Scaredy-T.E.D.

T.E.D. looks scared, but what is he running away from? Draw an alien to frighten him.

Spot the difference

There are five differences between these two pictures of Jim, Rover and Ripple. Can you spot them?

Answers: The image on the View Comm is missing; the Lunar Worm has appeared; Ripple's eyebrows are missing; the 4 coloured buttons on Ripple's suit are missing; the rocket image on Jim's cup has appeared.

Today's mission is to have fun!

Colour in this picture of Ripple on her Lunar Scooter.

Who's next?

Look at each line of pictures and say who comes next in each pattern.

Answer: Rover; Dolores; Ripple.

Super circles

There are lots of circle shapes in this picture of Jim in the Lunar Crawler. See how many you can find.

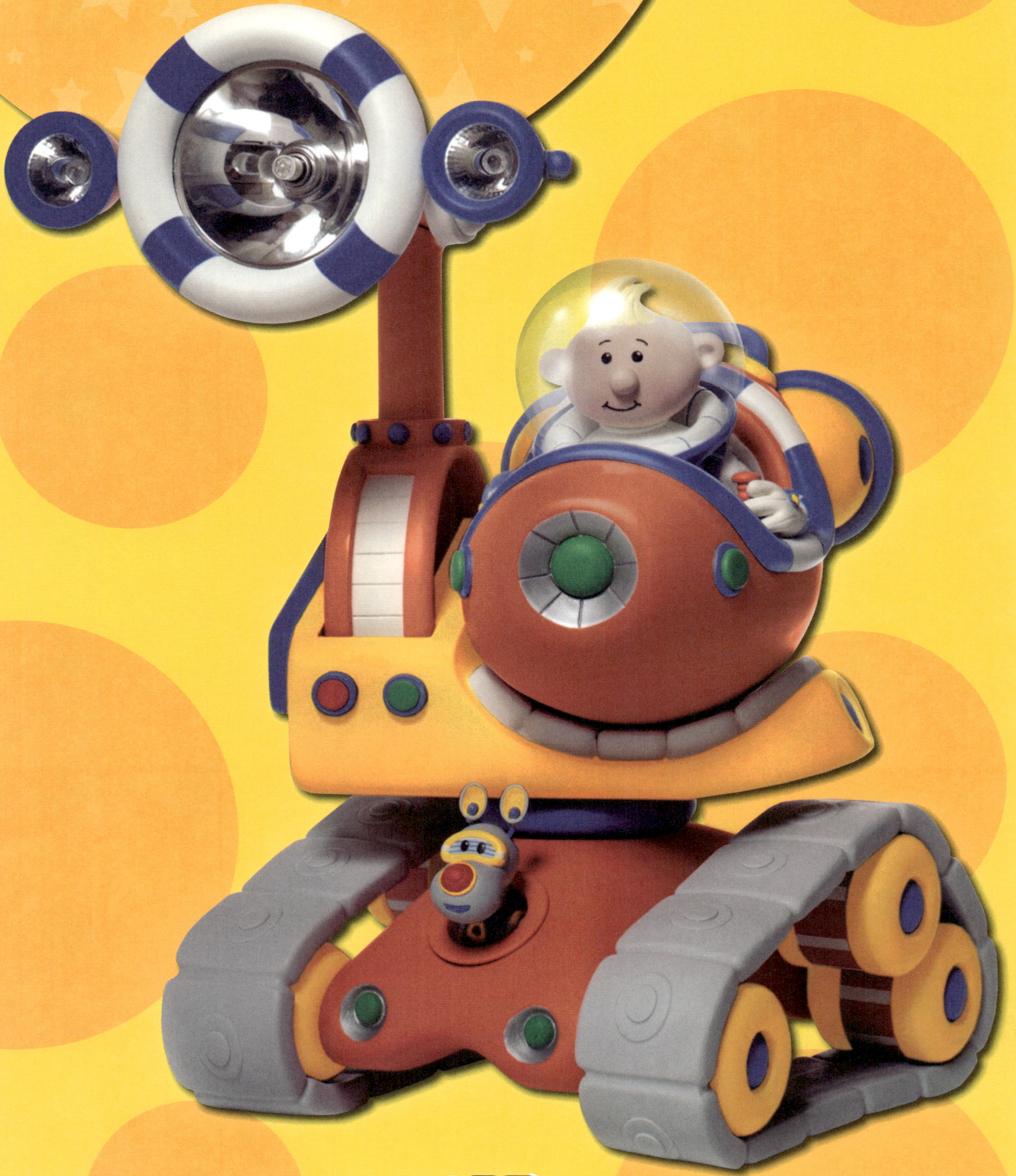

Odd Eco out

One of these pictures of Eco is different to all the others. Can you say which one it is?

A

B

C

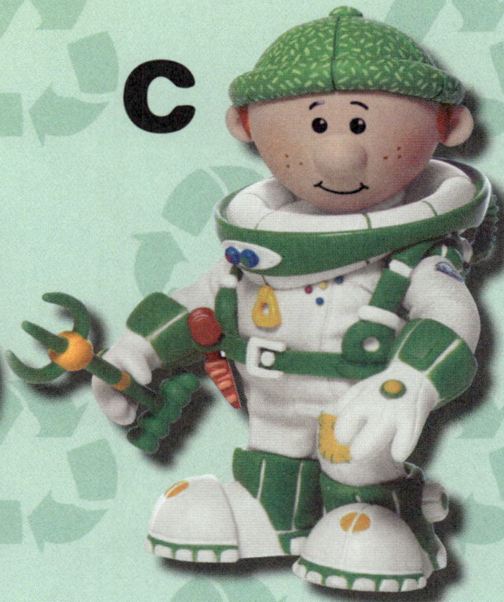

D

E

F

Answer: F. The freckles on Eco's face are missing.

Copy and colour Jim

Copy this picture of Jim into the grid on the opposite page.

Now colour your picture.

Shadow shapes

Can you match these objects to the shadows they make? Draw lines between the pairs.

Answers: 1-C; 2-D; 3-A; 4-B

View Comm zoom

The View Comm has zoomed in on some of the team. Can you help Jim identify them?

A

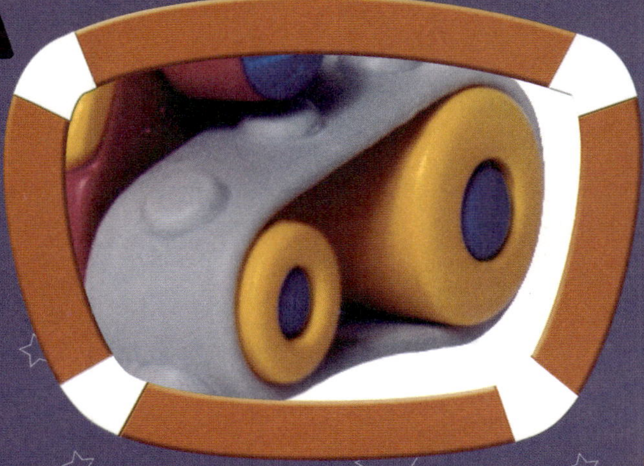

B

C

D

E

F

Answers: A Lunar Crawler; B Lunar Worm; C Rover; D Ripple; E Lunar Jim; F Eco.

Breakfast time in Moona Luna

Look at this big picture of Jim and Rover having their breakfast. Can you find all the items in the box below in the big picture?

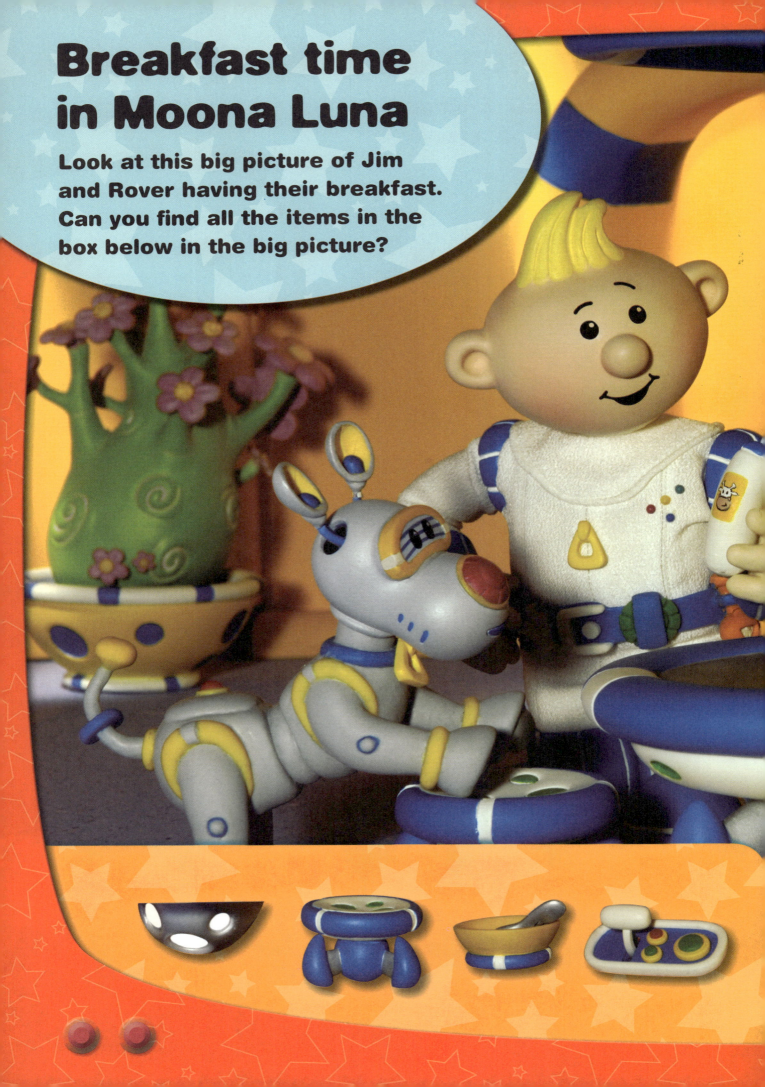

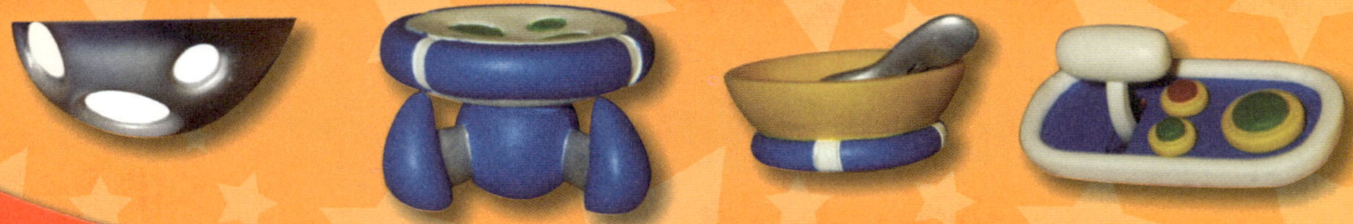

Eco's true or false

Look at the picture of Eco and say whether these statements are true or false.

1. Daisy and Dolores are in the Ecodome with Eco.

2. Eco is looking at the View Comm.

3. There are two moon melons in the picture.

4. Eco's hat is blue.

5. Daisy is wearing a hat, too.

Answer: 1. False, Dolores is not in the picture; 2. True, Eco is looking at the View Comm; 3. True, there are two moon melons; 4. False, Eco's hat is green; 5. False, Daisy is not wearing a hat.

Cosmic colours: yellow

There are many yellow things in Moona Luna. Look at these pictures and circle the ones that are yellow.

How many yellow things can you find in your house?

Answer: The following things are yellow - Rover's ball, the Lunar Lifter, Jim's Music Player.

Great Galaxies!

Colour in this picture of Jim and Rover in the Lunar Lifter.

Star mobile

When Jim looks through his telescope, he sees thousands of stars! Make your own star mobile to hang in your room.

You will need:
Tracing paper
Pencil
White card
Two 30cm sticks
Round-ended scissors
Glitter
String
Safe glue
A grown-up to help

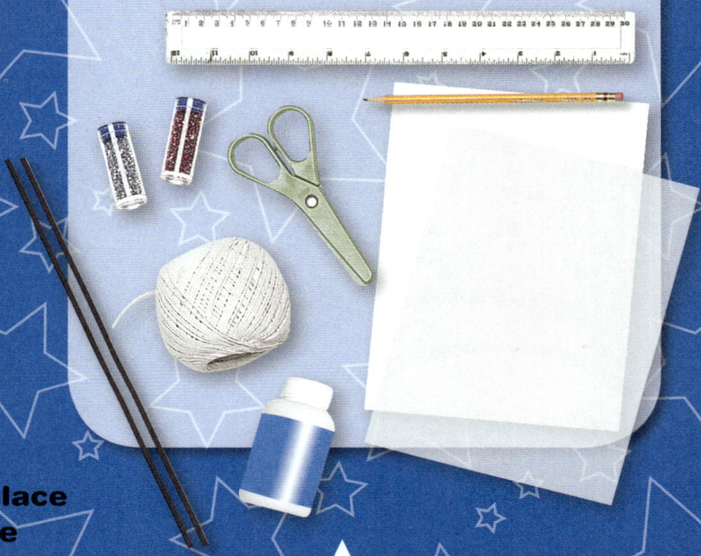

1 Place the tracing paper over the star template and copy over the lines in pencil. Turn the tracing paper over and scribble over the lines on the back. Now place the tracing paper the right way up over the white card. Pressing hard with the pencil, draw over the lines to make a star shape.

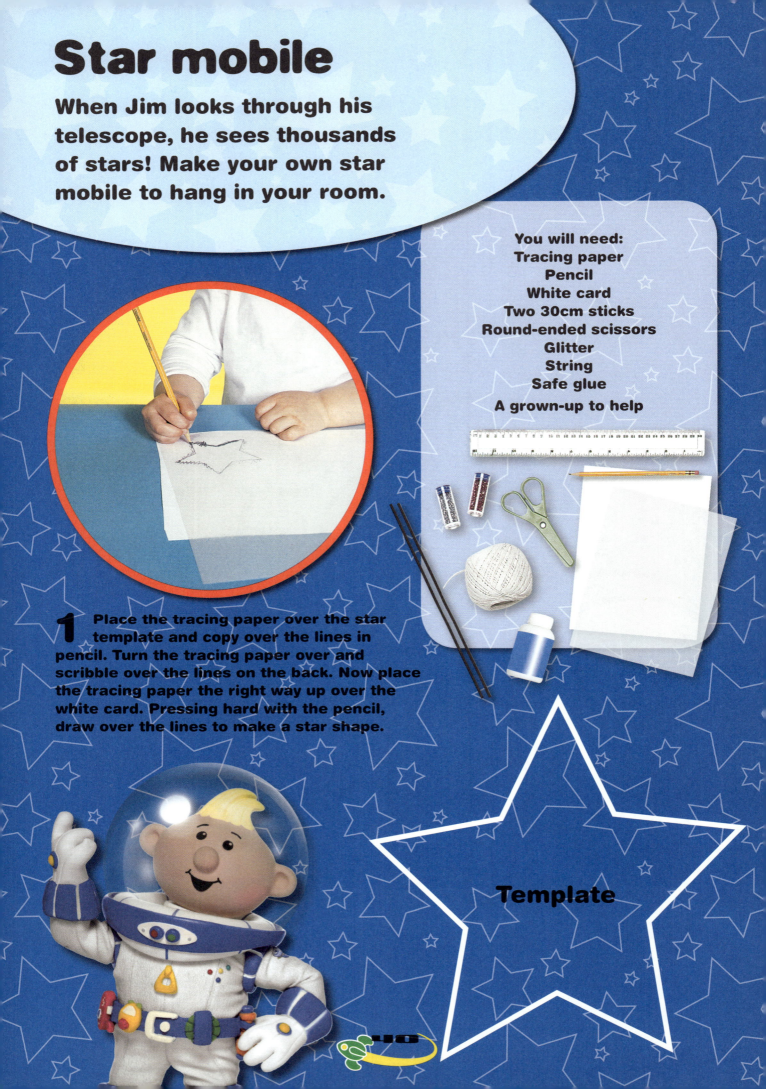

2 Make four star shapes on the card and cut them out.

3 Spread glue on one side of the stars.

4 Sprinkle glitter on the glue. When the first side is dry, turn each star over and do the same on the back.

5 Cross the sticks over each other and ask a grown-up to help you tie them together in the middle with string. Make sure there is an extra long piece of string to hang your mobile from.

6 Cut four 30cm pieces of string. Glue one end of each piece of string to a star. Tie the other ends to the ends of the sticks.

Now you can hang up your lunar star mobile!

Copy and colour Ripple

Copy this picture of Ripple into the grid on the opposite page.

Now colour your picture.

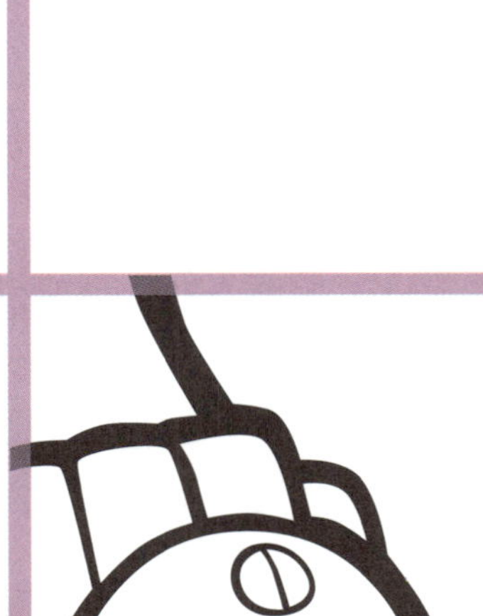

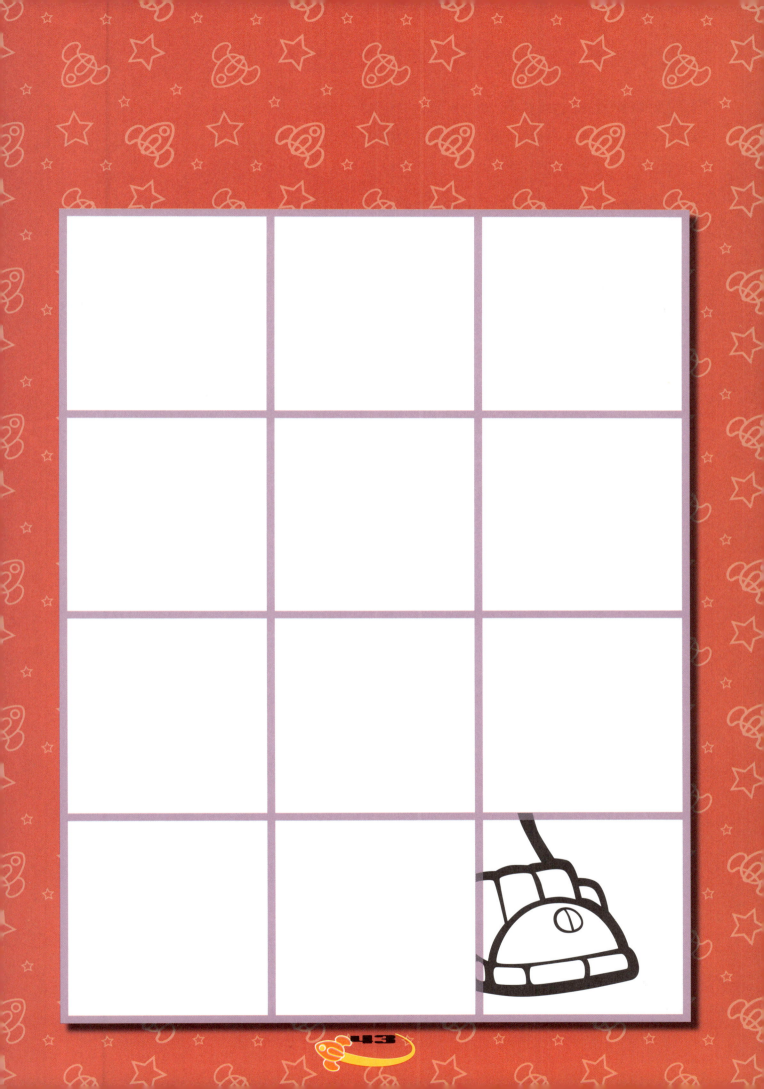

Moona Luna maze

Fly with Jim and Rover through the star maze to find Moona Luna.

Eco's crossword

Look at the picture clues, then fit the answers into the crossword.

3 DOWN

2 ACROSS

4 ACROSS

1 DOWN

3 ACROSS

Answers: 1 Down - melon; 3 Down - fork; 2 Across - gnome; 3 Across - flower; 4 Across - bucket.

Count and draw with Colby

Colby likes to collect things, but he has not got as many of each item as he thought. Draw in the extra ones, so the numbers are correct.

6

4

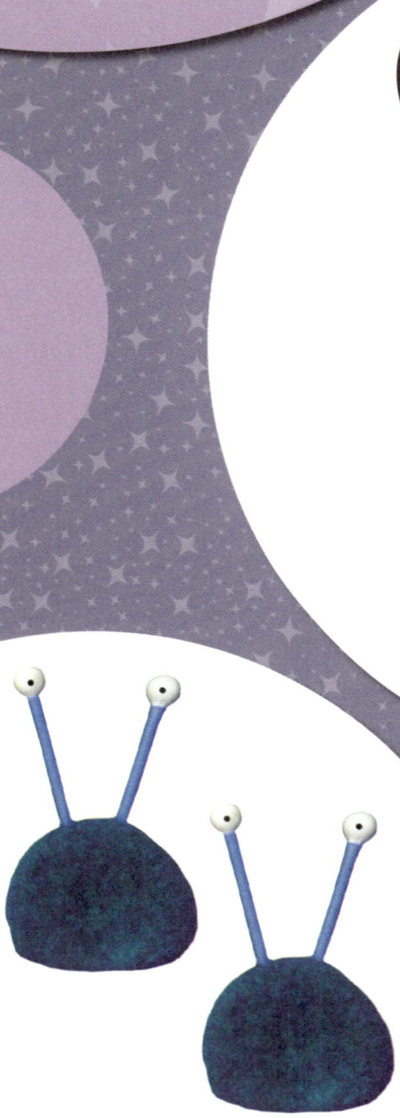

3

2

Lunar fun!

Colour in these pictures of Eco and Jim on their Lunar vehicles.

Memory game

Look carefully at this picture of Jim and the gang, then turn the page and see how many questions you can answer.

What can you remember?

1. What is Jim holding?

2. Who is missing from the picture?

3. What colour is Eco's hat?

4. How many blue flowers are there?

5. Is Dolores wearing a space suit?

Answers: 1. A blue jumper;
2. Ripple and T.E.D.; 3. Green;
4. Two; 5. Yes.

Jumble words

All the letters in these names have got muddled up! Can you unscramble them?

E D T

C E O

M I J

P I L P R E

O V R E R

Answers: T.E.D., Eco, Jim, Ripple, Rover.

Toolbox tidy up

Help Ripple tidy up her tools. Draw a line from the tools to their shadows.

Bleep blip!

Colour in Rover.

Flower fun

Eco is growing some strange flowers in the Ecodome. Draw some more interesting plants in his garden, then colour the picture.

Spot the difference

Look carefully at these two pictures of T.E.D. and the Lunar Worm. Can you spot five differences between them?

Answers: The crater in the top left of the picture is missing; there is a new rock on the ground; T.E.D.'s righthand fingers are missing; the buttons on T.E.D.'s chest are a different colour; the Lunar Worm's eyes are missing their pupils.

Star-gazing

Join the dots to reveal what Jim can see through his telescope.

Moona Luna muddle

Can you help Jim, Eco and Ripple find their ways home? Follow the wiggly lines to lead them to their houses.

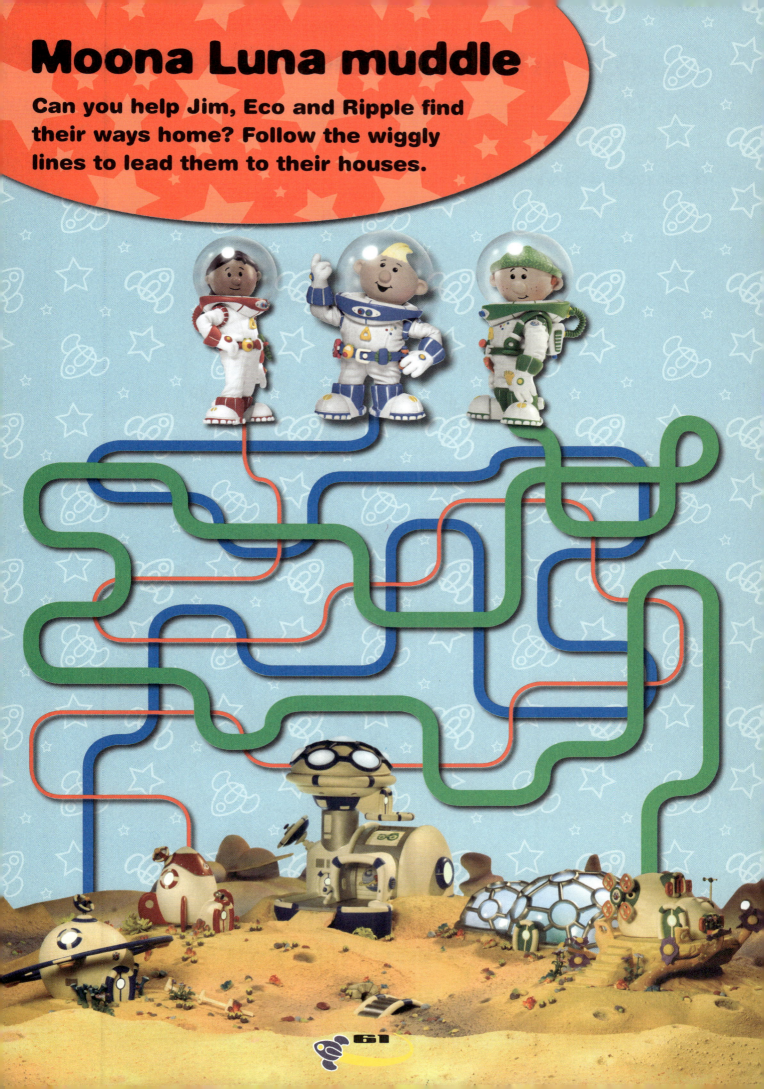

Copy and colour T.E.D.

Copy this picture of T.E.D. into the grid on the opposite page.

Now colour your picture.

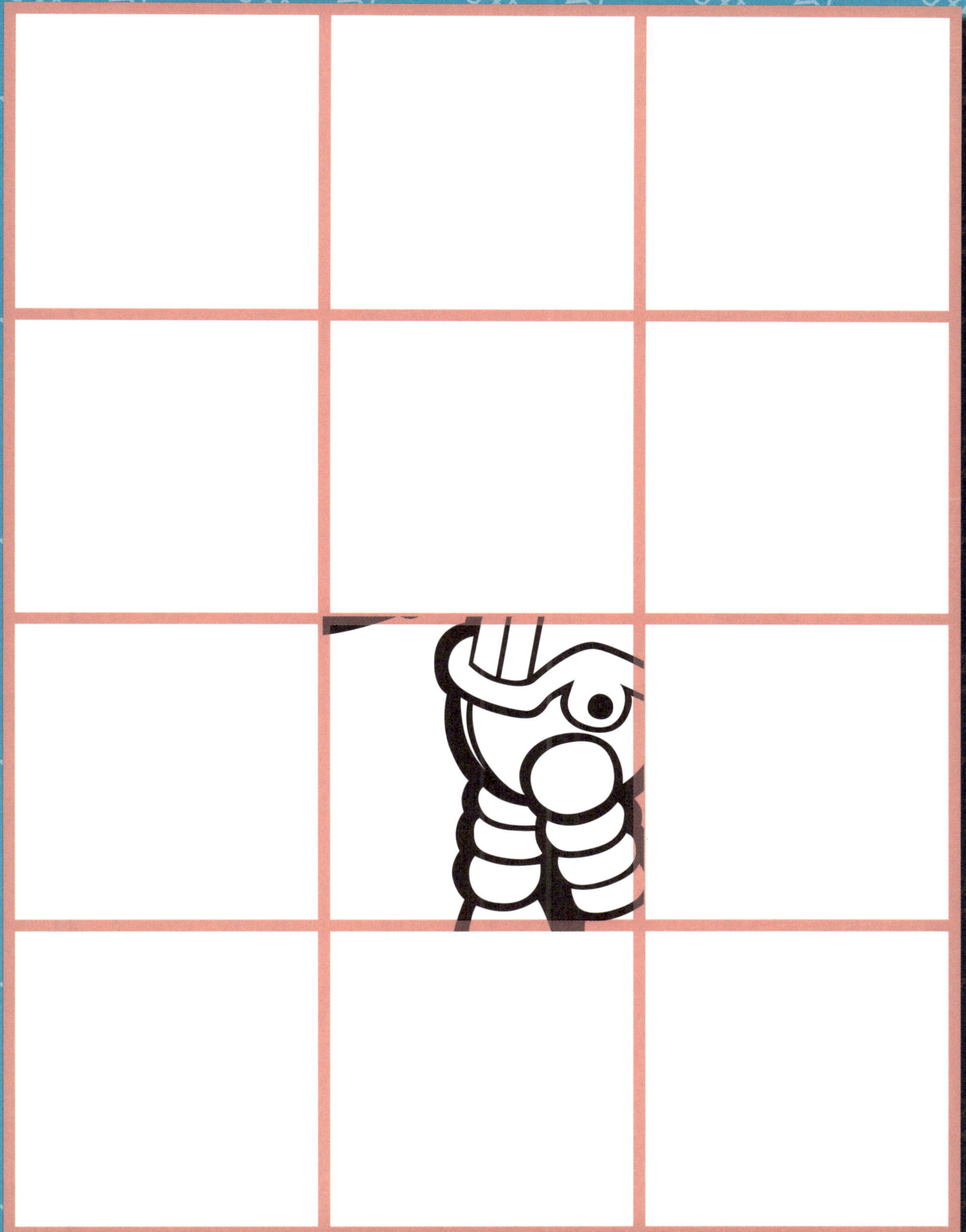

Odd Colby out

One of these pictures of Colby is different to the others. Draw a circle around the odd Colby out.

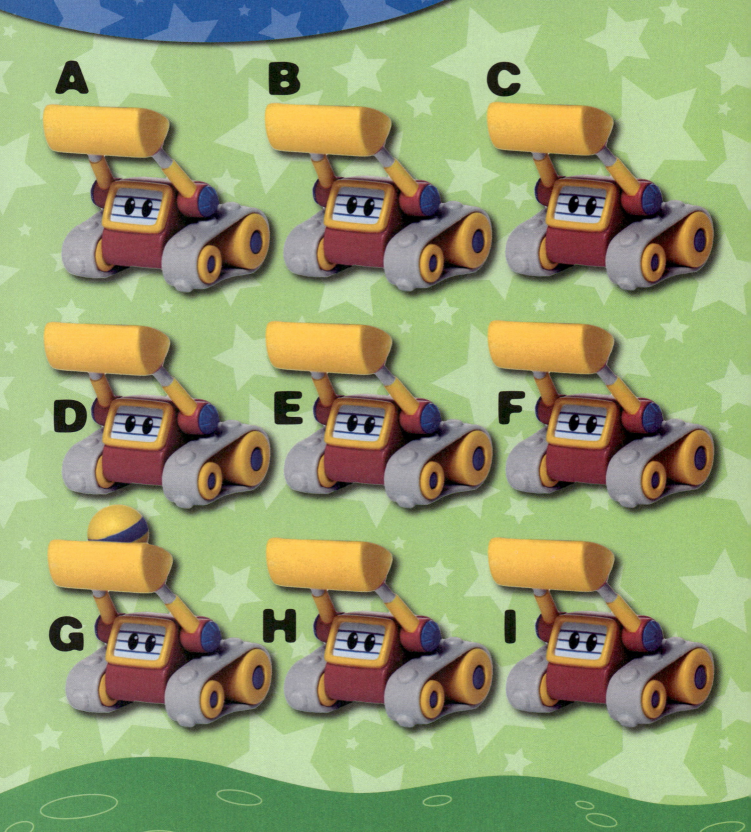

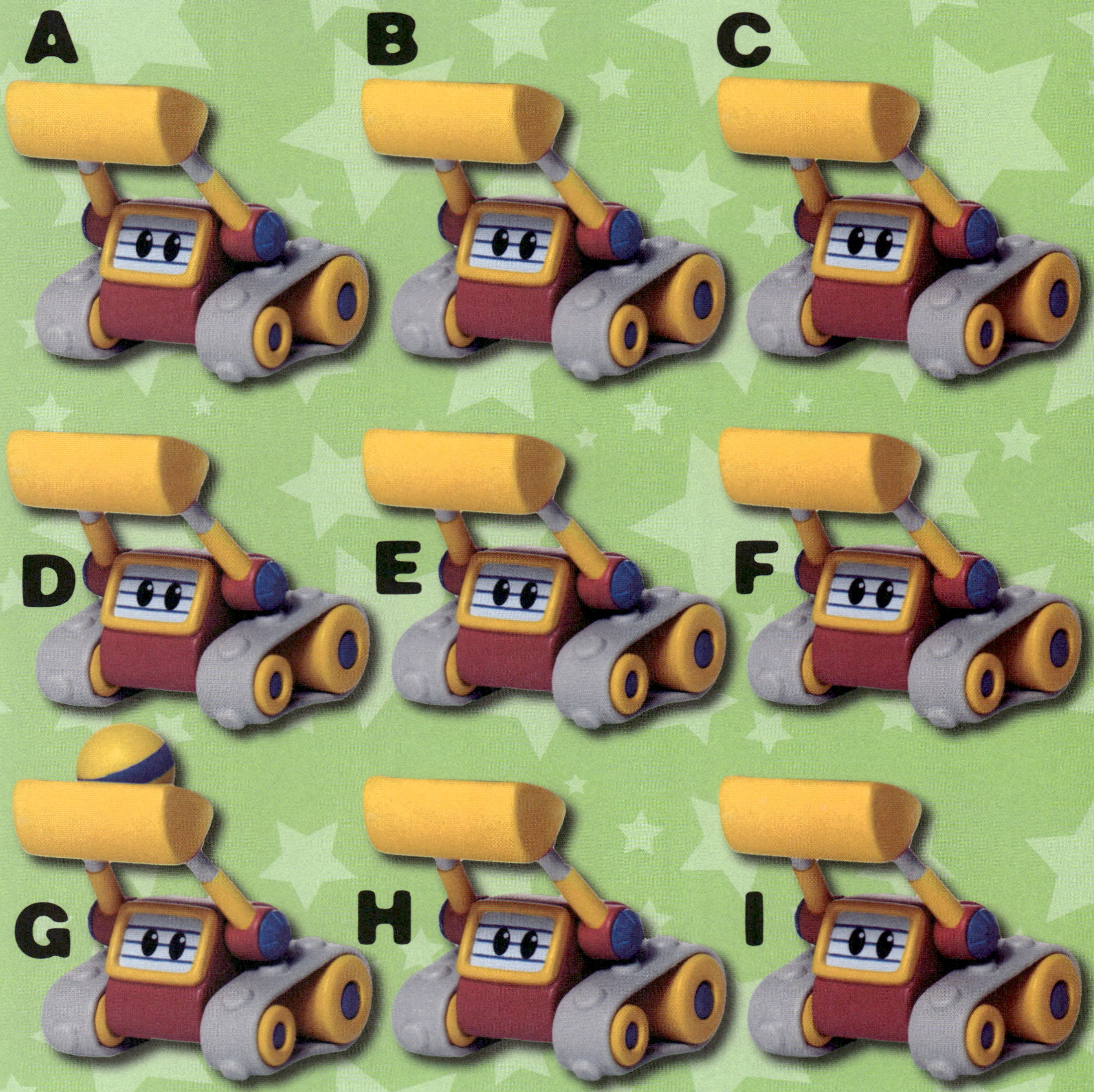

Answer: G - Colby has Rover's ball in his scoop.

Vehicle wordsearch

There are five vehicle words hidden up and down, from side to side and diagonally in this wordsearch. Can you find them?

Hopper

Scrambler

Lifter

Scooter

Crawler

S	C	R	A	M	B	L	E	R
O	R	C	L	P	U	B	O	H
R	A	P	Z	I	D	C	W	V
S	W	Q	P	U	F	Y	T	X
K	L	I	C	O	B	T	M	S
O	E	N	H	O	P	P	E	R
I	R	N	S	I	U	A	P	R
S	C	O	O	T	E	R	G	H

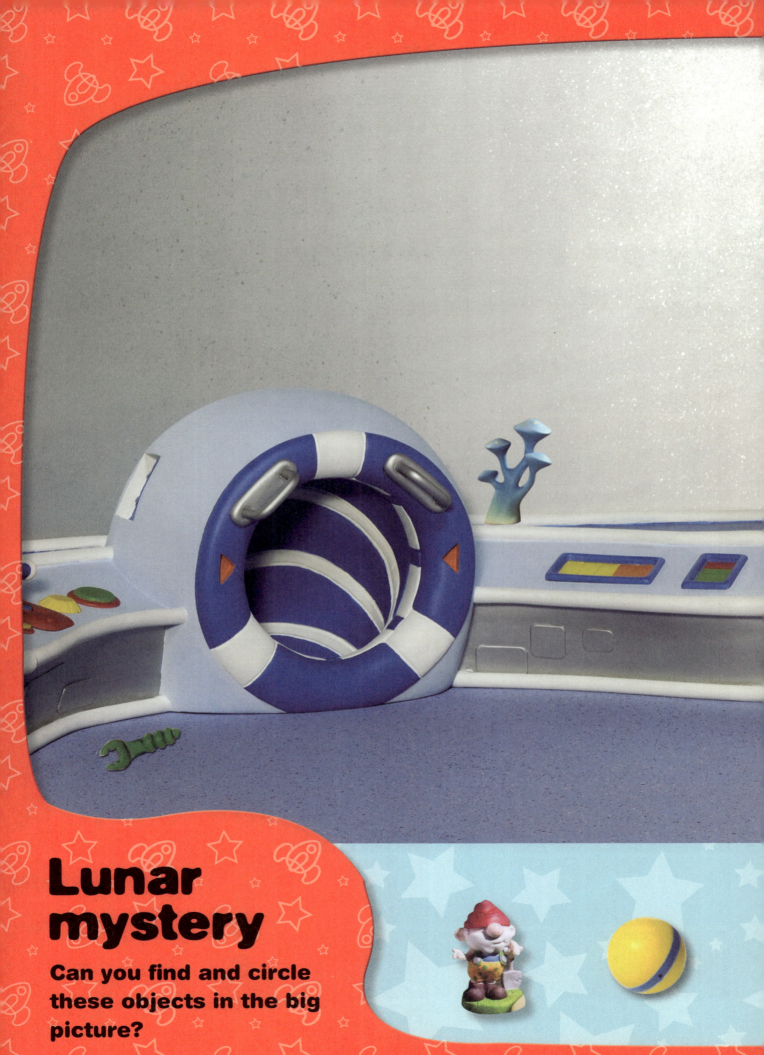

Lunar mystery

Can you find and circle these objects in the big picture?

Ripple's true or false

Look at the picture of Ripple and say whether these statements are true or false.

1. Ripple is not wearing her helmet.

2. The Lunar Worm is green.

3. Jim is in the picture, too.

4. Ripple's Lunar Scooter is blue.

5. There are pink flowers in the lunar landscape.

Answers: 1. False, Ripple is wearing her helmet; 2. True, the Lunar Worm is green; 3. False, Jim is not in the picture; 4. False, Ripple's Lunar Scooter is red; 5. False, there are no pink flowers.

Guess who?

Look at the pictures of Jim and the gang, then draw a line to the shadows they make.

Cosmic colours: red

There are many red things in Moona Luna. Look at these pictures and circle the ones that are red.

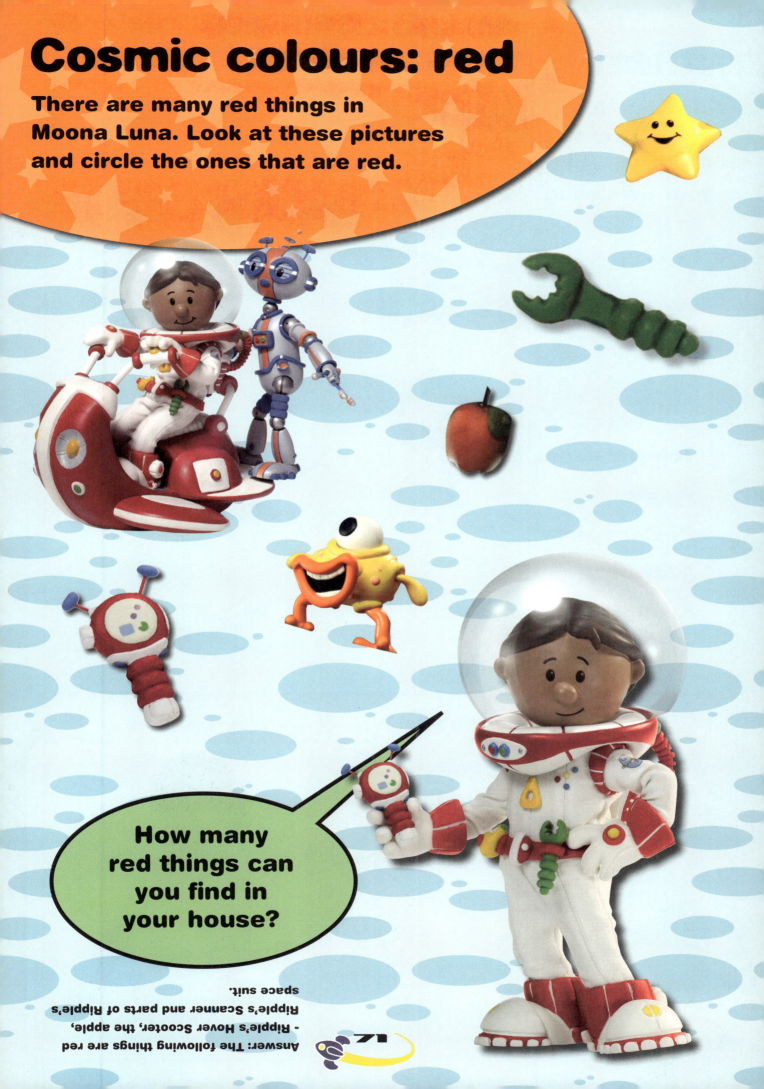

How many red things can you find in your house?

Answer: The following things are red - Ripple's Hover Scooter, the apple, Ripple's Scanner and parts of Ripple's space suit.

Alien blow-painting

Jim and his friends find all sorts of funny creatures on the Moon. Follow these instructions to make your own alien blow-paintings.

You will need:

Paper

Poster paints

A straw

Round-ended scissors

Safety glue

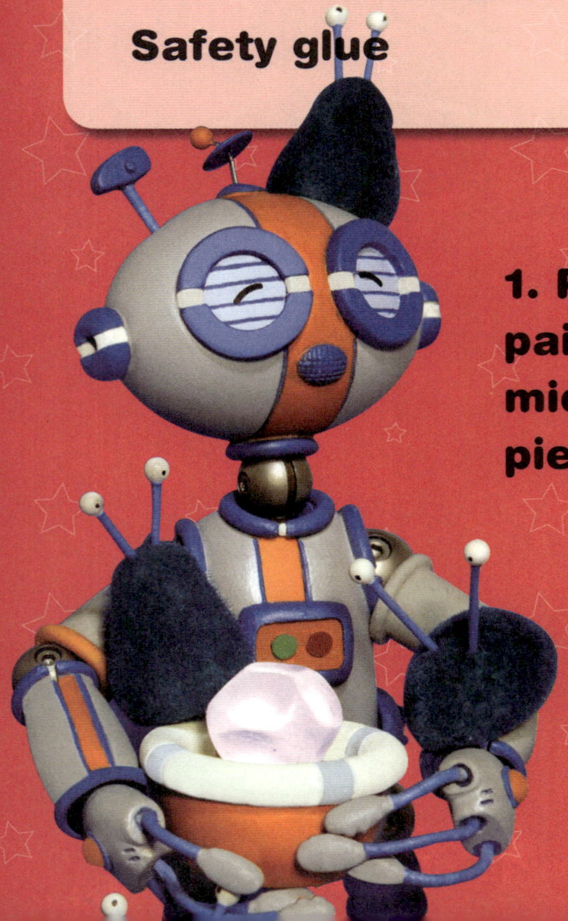

1. Pour some paint into the middle of a piece of paper.

2. Point the straw at the paint and gently blow through it. Move the straw around to make different shapes.

3. Wait for the paint to dry, then carefully cut out your alien.

These aliens look a little bit like the Lunar Fluffies that live in Moona Luna.

4. Cut out some eyes and a mouth, and glue them to make a face.

What do your aliens look like?

Space race!

You will need:

A counter for each player

A die

Race back to Moona Luna by taking turns to roll the die and move around the board. The first player home is the winner!

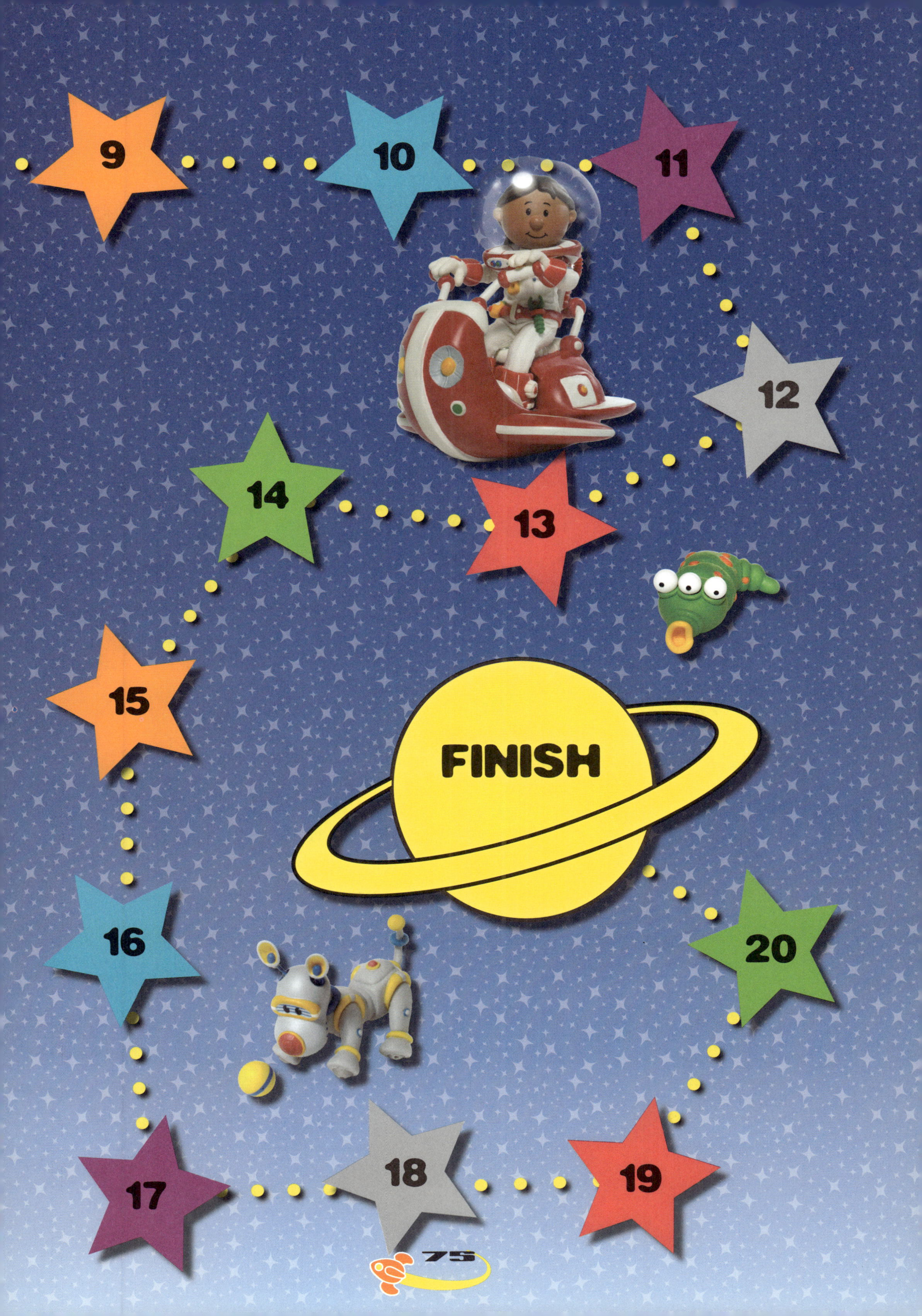
9
10
11
12
13
14
15
16
17
18
19
20
FINISH

Crashing Comets!

Colour in this picture of Eco, Rover and T.E.D..

Pixel's pictures

Pixel is trying to show pictures of the team, but they have got muddled up. Draw a line to connect the tops and bottoms of the pictures.

What's next?

Look at the box at the bottom of the page, then say which object is missing from each pattern.

Answer: Music Player, Lunar Fluffy, Lunar plant.

Ripple's pairs

Look at the six pictures of Ripple below. Draw lines between the matching pairs.

1

2

3

A

B

C

Answer: 1-A, 2-C, 3-B.

View Comm view

The View Comm is showing the team the lunar landscape. Draw something that they can see.

Copy and colour Eco

Copy this picture of Eco into the grid on the opposite page.

Now colour your picture.

Blue banana maze

Help the Lunar Worm to find his way through the maze, collecting all the blue bananas as you go.

Comet counting

Count the comets in each row and say how many there are. Write the number in the circle.

Answer: 2, 5, 3, 6.

Mission Control

Look at the big picture of Ripple and T.E.D. in Mission Control. Can you find all the objects below in the big picture?

Circle all these objects when you find them.

Let's Get Lunar!

Colour the pictures of Jim, Rover, Ripple and T.E.D..

Odd Jim out

One of these pictures of Jim is different to the others. Can you spot it? Draw a circle around the odd Jim out.

A

B

C

D

E

F

Answer: D - the coloured buttons on Jim's suit are missing.

Fruit confusion

Eco has forgotten to label all the fruits he is growing. Help him by drawing lines to match the labels to the plants.

1

2

3

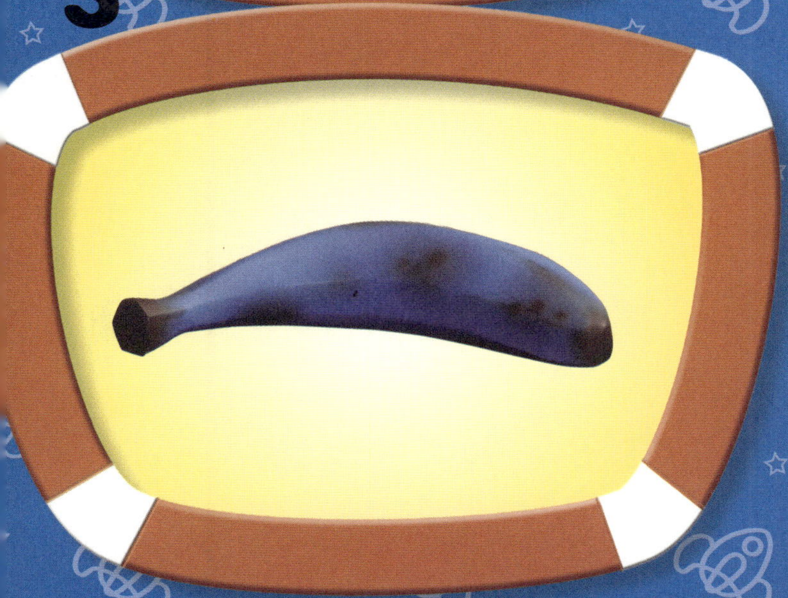

MOON MELON

BLUE MOON BANANA

APPLES

Answers: 1 Apples; 2 Moon melon; 3 Blue moon banana.

Rover's true or false

Look at the picture of Rover and say whether these statements are true or false.

1. Rover has a red nose.

2. There are three trees in the picture.

3. Rover is sitting down.

4. Eco's wheelbarrow is full of blue Moon bananas.

5. The grass in the Ecodome is purple.

Answers: 1. True, Rover does have a red nose; 2. True, there are three trees in the picture; 3. False, Rover is standing up; 4. False, Eco's wheelbarrow is full of Moon melons; 5. False, the grass in the Ecodome is green.

Cosmic colours: green

There are many green things in Moona Luna. Look at these pictures and circle the ones that are green.

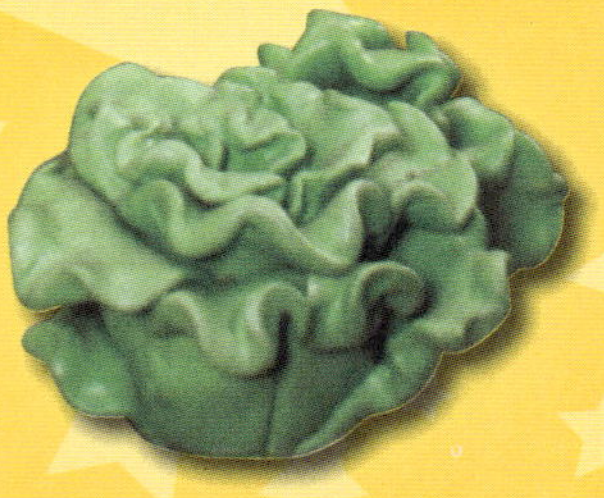

How many green things can you find in your house?

Answer: The following things are green - the pitchfork, the lettuce, Ripple's spanner, Eco's hat and parts of his space suit.

Colby's commotion

Colby has been collecting everyone's things and now they are all jumbled up! Draw lines to match the objects to their owners.

Answer: Ripple - Scanner; Jim - Music Player; Eco - pitchfork.

Lunar animals

Colour in this picture of Daisy and Dolores.

Space suits

Jim and Ripple need new space suits. Draw them some new clothes, then colour the picture.

Eco's wordsearch

There are five Ecodome words hidden up and down, from side to side and diagonally in this wordsearch. Can you find them?

C	Y	D	X	Q	I	S	O	L
Q	H	Y	H	N	B	P	I	W
W	V	I	O	N	K	A	M	M
C	O	W	C	B	R	D	A	E
S	L	Q	S	K	I	E	V	L
X	G	N	O	M	E	Y	S	O
		X	T	R	A	N	W	N

Space face masks

You will need:
A piece of card for each mask
Round-ended scissors
Tracing paper
A pencil
Colouring pencils or crayons
Ribbon or string
Sticky tape
A grown-up to help

1. If you don't want to cut up your book, place some tracing paper over the mask outlines on the next page and copy over the lines with your pencil. Turn the tracing paper over and scribble over the lines on the back. Now place the tracing paper the right way up over the white card. Pressing hard with the pencil, draw over the lines to make the mask shape.

2. Ask a grown-up to help you cut around the mask, and to cut out the eyeholes and the holes for the string.

3. Colour in your mask.

4. Tie a piece of ribbon or string through the holes on each side of your mask, and ask a grown-up to help you tie on your mask.

5. Now you can play at being Jim or T.E.D.!

T.E.D.'s mask

Jim's mask

Lunar friends

Colour in Jim and the gang.

Big and small

Look at the objects below and answer each question.

Which is the biggest Crater Critter?

Which is the smallest Dolores?

Which is the longest pitchfork?

Answers: C is the biggest Crater Critter! B is the smallest Dolores; A is the longest pitchfork.

Lunar adventure

The gang are getting into pairs to go exploring. Follow the wiggly lines to see who goes together.

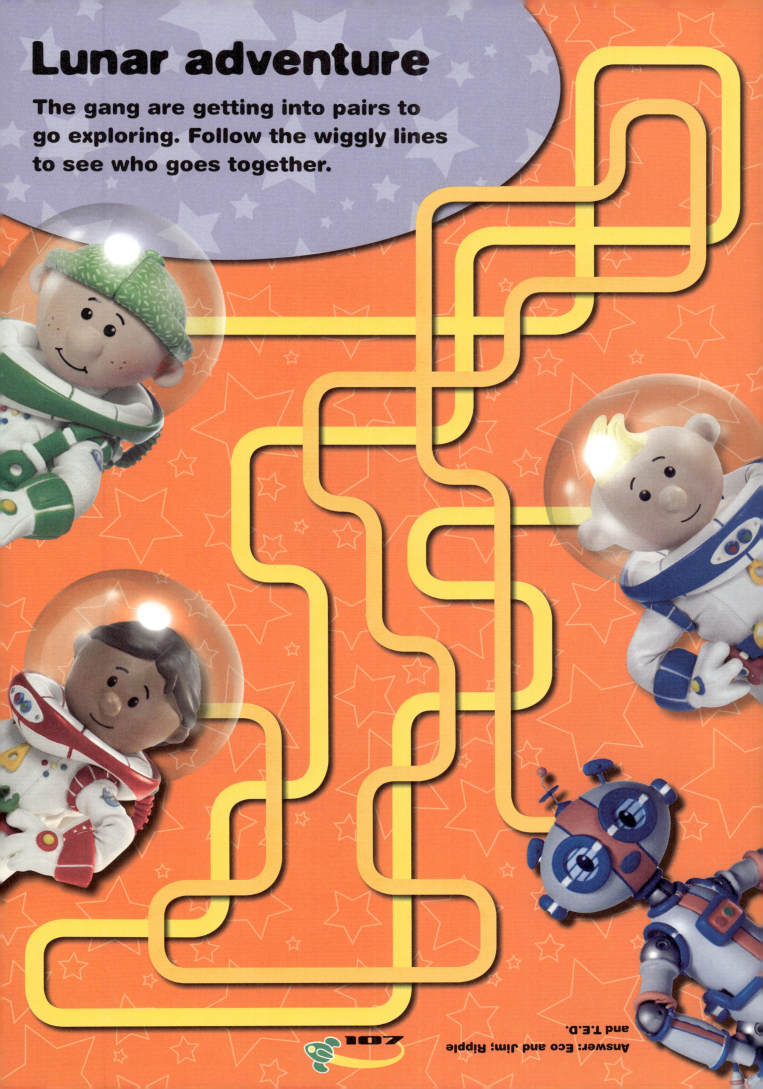

Answer: Eco and Jim; Ripple and T.E.D.

Spot the difference

Look carefully at these two pictures in the Ecodome. Can you circle five differences in the second one?

Answers: The inside of the inflated tent is a different colour; the green button on the tent entrance arch is missing; the gnome has appeared; the Garden Bot's eyes are missing; one of the lettuces is missing.

Freaky fruit

Eco is searching for new fruits in Moona Luna. Help him by drawing some strange new fruits below.

Space snap

Jim has been playing snap. Draw a line between the pictures that match.

A

B

C

D

E

F

G

H

I

J

K

L

Answers: A - G; B - D; C - H; E - J; F - L; I - K.

Copy and colour Rover

Copy this picture of Rover into the grid on the opposite page.

Now colour your picture.

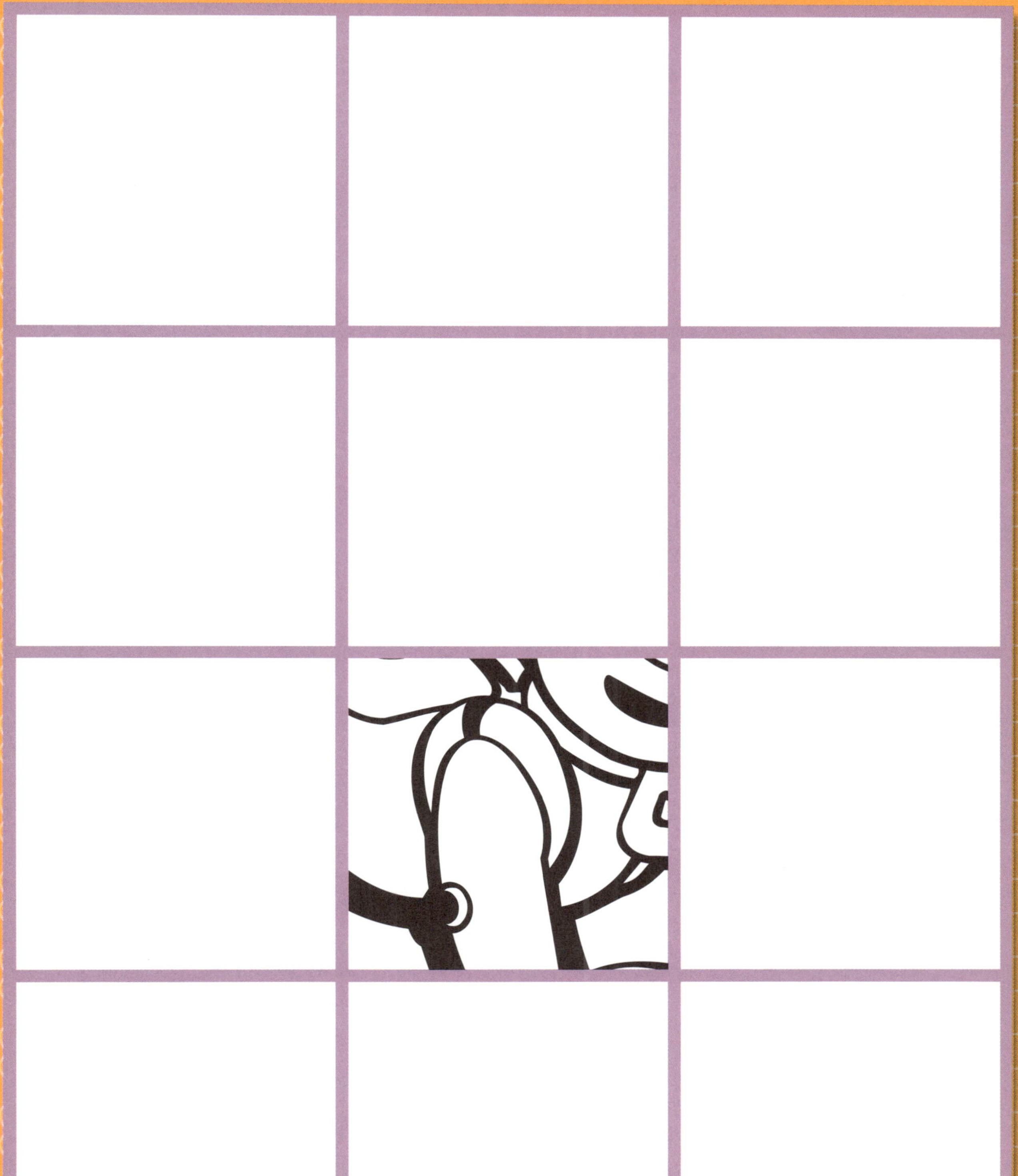

Cosmic colours: orange

There are many orange things in Moona Luna. Look at these pictures and circle the ones that are orange.

How many orange things can you find in your house?

Answer: The following things are orange - the spade, Rover's space pod, parts of T.E.D. and Dolores face and wings.

Fly me to the moon

Jim needs a new space rocket. Draw him one in the space below.

Memory game

Look carefully at this picture of Eco and Daisy, then turn the page and see how many questions you can answer.

What can you remember?

1. How many corn cobs are there in the supply pod?

2. What is Daisy wearing around her neck?

3. How many buttons are there on the door of the Ecodome?

4. What is Eco holding?

5. What colour are Eco's moon boots?

Answers: 1. There are four corn cobs in the supply pod; 2. Daisy has a bell around her neck; 3. There are two buttons on the door; 4. Eco is holding a bowl of popcorn; 5. Eco's moon boots are green.

Fluffies maze

Jim is taking the Lunar Fluffies home to Crystal Cave. Help Jim find his way through the maze, collecting the Fluffies as you go.

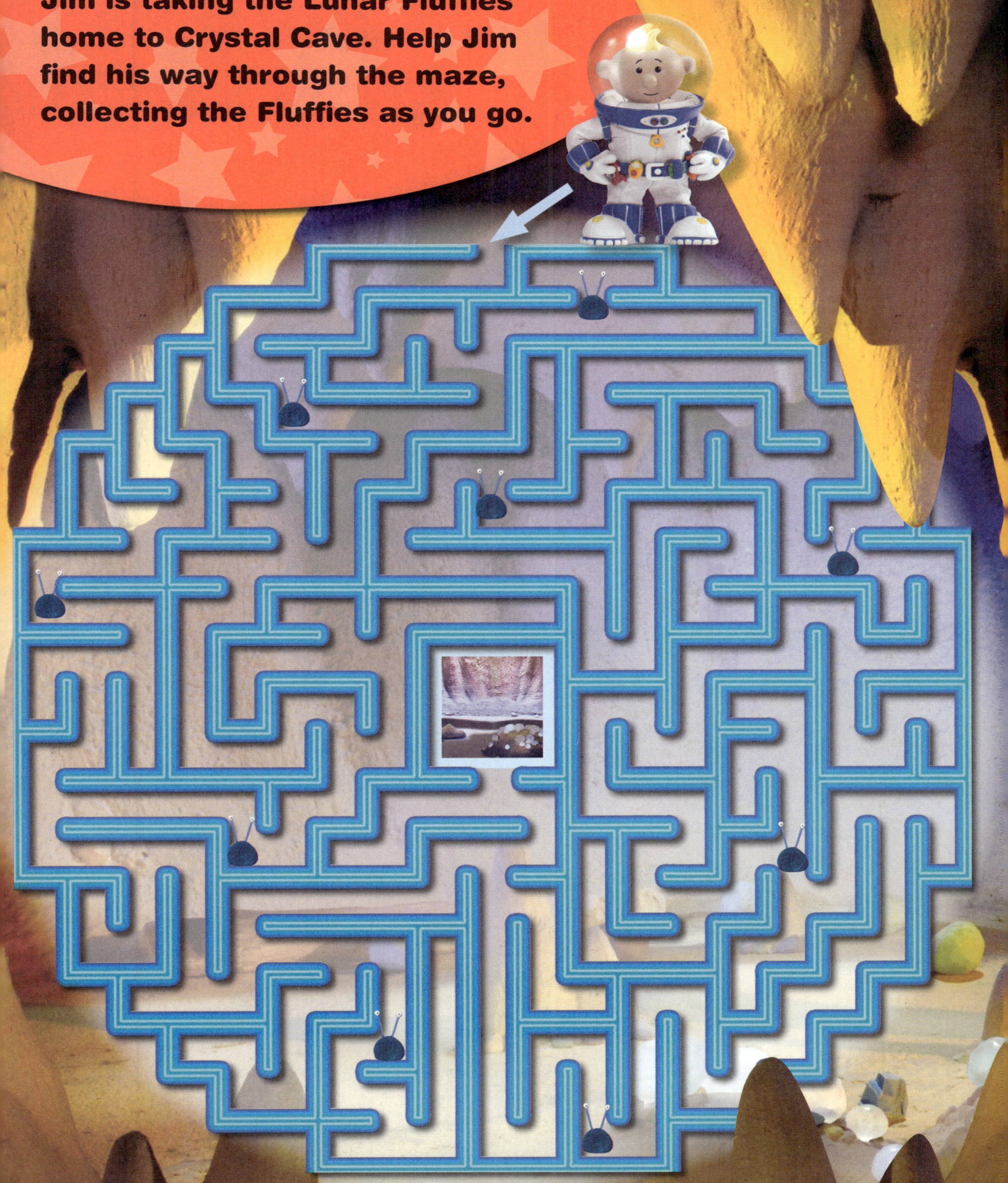

Gnome trouble

There are gnomes all over the Ecodome! See how many you can find.

Answer: There are six gnomes hidden in the picture.

T.E.D.'s true or false

Look at the picture of T.E.D. and say whether these statements are true or false.

1. T.E.D. is carrying a crystal.
2. The door behind T.E.D. is open.
3. There are six Lunar Fluffies in the picture.
4. T.E.D. has an orange stripe on his face.
5. The Lunar Fluffies are green.

Answers: 1. True, T.E.D. is carrying a crystal; 2. False, the door behind T.E.D. is closed; 3. True, there are six Lunar Fluffies in the picture; 4. True, T.E.D. has an orange stripe on his face; 5. False, the Lunar Fluffies are blue, not green.

Whose toes are those?

Draw lines to match the characters' names to their feet.

B

C

A

ECO

ROVER

RIPPLE

DAISY

JIM

T.E.D

E

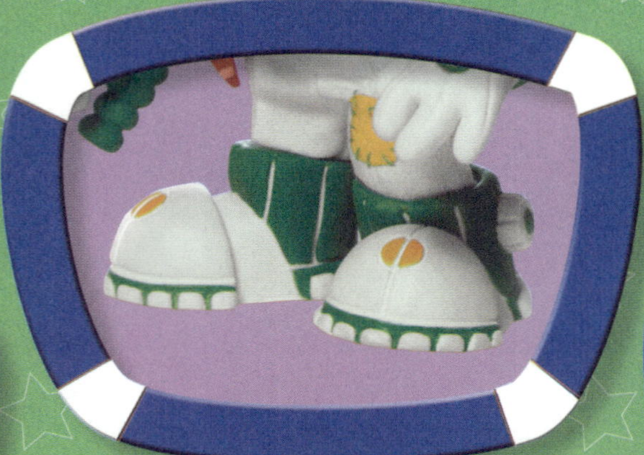

F

D

Answers: A - T.E.D.; B - Ripple; C - Jim; D - Rover; E - Eco; F - Daisy.

Counting cows

How many pictures of Daisy can you count?

Answer: 18

Space rakes and lunar ladders

You will need:
A die
A counter for each player

Take turns to roll the die and move around the board. If you land on a ladder, climb up to the square it finishes on. If you land on a rake, slide down to the bottom of it. The first player to reach the end is the winner.

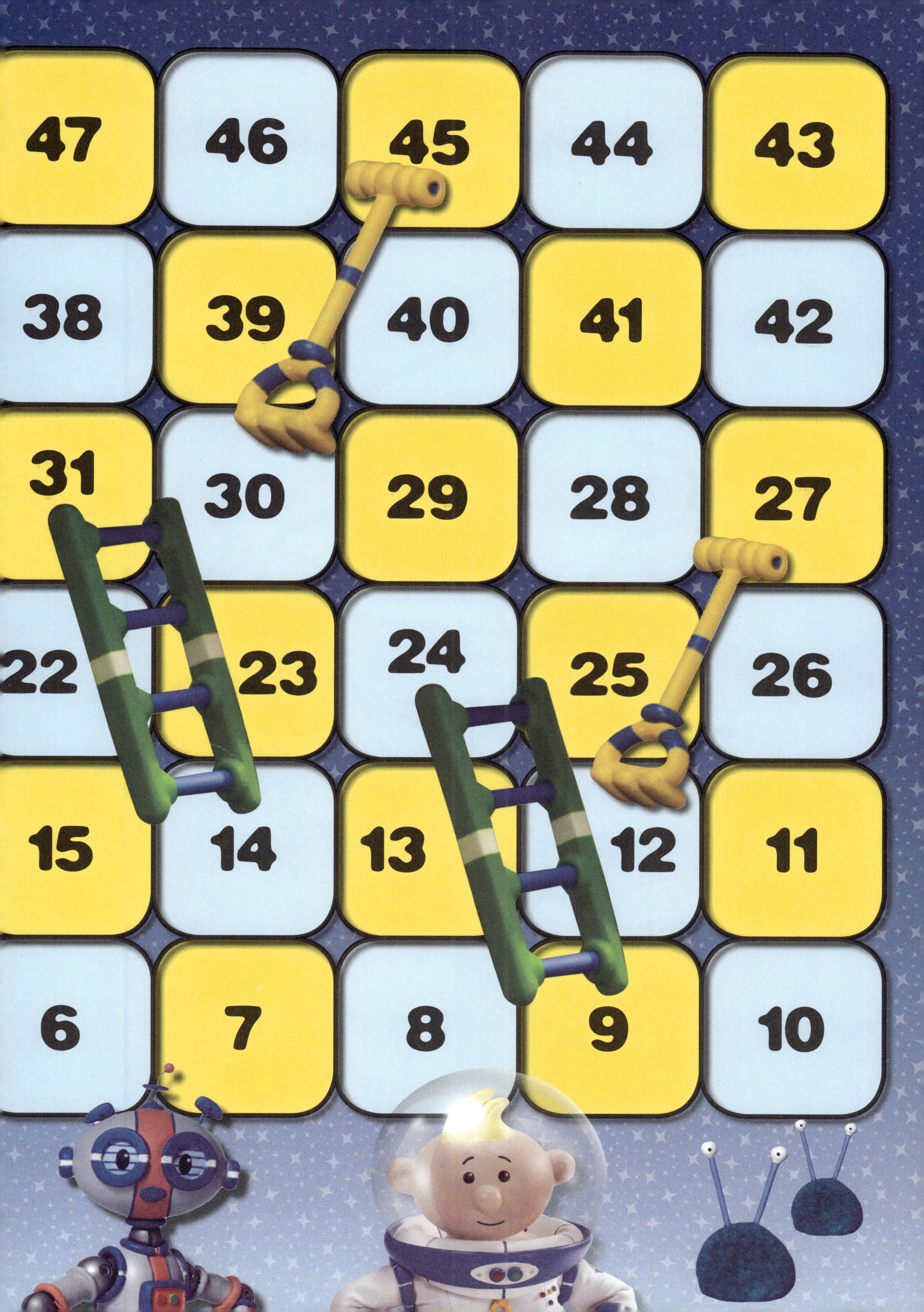

47
46
45
44
43
38
39
40
41
42
31
30
29
28
27
22
23
24
25
26
15
14
13
12
11
6
7
8
9
10

Let's Get Lunar!